Bible Explorers
Welcome to the World of

Dear Reader,

The Wizzy Gizmo series is more than fun-filled stories. It is an in-depth exposition of the Bible, book-by-book. Yes, it is filled with fun stories, but never will we compromise on accurately following the text of God's Word. Why? Because we believe:

> **"All Scripture is inspired by God and profitable for teaching, for reproof, for correction, for training in righteousness, that the man of God may be adequate, equipped for every good work."**
>
> **II Timothy 3:16,17**

Wizzy Gizmo

Old Testament Series - Book Two

In His Image

Written by:
Kirstin Del Aguila and Justin Cummins
General Editor: Dr. David Beverly

Illustrated by:
Justin Cummins & Angela Matlashevsky

EOG Studios, Publisher

This is a work of fiction and non-fiction. The Wizzy Gizmo characters, places, and incidents are either products of the authors imagination or, if real are used fictitiously.

Written by: Kirstin Del Aguila and Justin Cummins
Cover by: Justin Cummins
General Editor: Dr. David Beverly
Illustrations by: Justin Cummins and Angela Matlashevsky

Text copyright © 2014 EOG Studios
Illustrations copyright © 2014 EOG Studios

First paperback edition 2014

All rights reserved. No part of this publication may be reproduced, transmitted or stored in an information retrieval system in any form or by any means, graphic, electronic, or mechanical, including photocopying, taping and recording, without prior written permission from the publisher. The only exception is brief quotation in printed reviews.
EOG Studios: info@eogstudios.com

Wizzy Gizmo names, characters, and related indicia are copyright, trademark, and exclusive license of EOG Studios.

Library of Congress Catalog-in-Publication Data
EOG Studios, 2014 Wizzy Gizmo Old Testament Series Book Two:
In His Image

Summary: The kids of Sunnyville experience an incredible adventure as they watch God create the first man and woman.

ISBN-10: 0989824535
ISBN-13: 978-0-9898245-3-8

Scripture taken from the NEW AMERICAN STANDARD BIBLE ®, COPYRIGHT © 1960, 1962, 1963, 1968, 1971, 1972, 1973, 1975, 1977, 1995 by the Lockman Foundation, used by permission.
www.Lockman.org

Printed in the U.S.A.

Additional resources available at www.wizzygizmo.com

CONTENTS

Excitement Awaits   7

Picnic Mayhem   11

Wondrous and Tasty Inventions   15

Creative Like the Creator   19

A Perfect World   25

Plants, Plants, Plants   33

In His Image   37

Review Questions   54

Vocabulary   56

Wizzy Gizmo is a world famous inventor and Professor of Science and Technology at Sunnyville University. Possibly his most significant invention is Gizmovision, a device which brings any book to life with the touch of a button.

Qwacky is a robotic duck that can't quite seem to figure out how to be a proper duck. He thinks he is a dog, or a tiger, or a lion, or maybe a parrot, or even an eagle. This problem is compounded by the fact that he can transform into anything he wants.

Pepe, whose full name is actually Praxedis López Ramos, is Wizzy Gizmo's pet dog. He has an advantage over other dogs, because he can think and speak through an invention Wizzy likes to call, *the Anama-Gizmo-Logic.*

Summer is the oldest, most reserved and mature of the Sunnyville kids. Age 9, she's always concerned about everyone's safety and wellbeing. She loves to read and is always ready to share from her wealth of knowledge.

Thomas is outgoing and fun. He loves to do adventurous things and is bursting with energy. He tends to find himself in extraordinary situations. He loves to play guitar and ride his skateboard. He is 7.

Eli is shy, but very observant. He loves history and science and wants to be a pilot or astronaut one day. He has a fascination for rockets and builds them as a hobby. He is 8.

Olive never walks, she runs, and barefoot at that. Age 7, she loves animals and is always chasing them, trying to hold them and pet them. She loves the outdoors, rivers, parks, mountains, etc.

CHAPTER 1

Excitement Awaits

Something odd and peculiar was happening in the Sanderson's cozy little living room. It was dizzying to watch. Like a ball bouncing from wall to wall, or a deer jumping from place to place, a figure moved from the couch to the chair to the floor and back again, left, right, forwards and back. This figure however, was not a deer or ball. No, not at all, it was Olive. Bursting with excitement, she jumped, danced, even pranced around the living room, her red curls bouncing up and down, her hands raised high in the air. She shouted in excitement, "It's Tuesday! It's Tuesday! Hooray for Tuesday!"

"Why is Tuesday so special?" asked Olive's mom.

Olive turned to her mom, and with a twinkle in her eye she said, "We're going to Wizzy Gizmo's, and we are going to have a picnic and see his new invention and it's going to be amazing and I just, I just…well, that is why today is so special."

"Oh, I see. That does sound like a lot of fun," her mother responded.

Olive finally came to a stop. She plopped herself down, hunched over the back of her big brown couch, and rested her elbows on the window ledge. She gazed into

the front yard, and watched as large golden leaves floated down from the old oak tree and landed softly on the grass-covered ground. The tire swing swayed gently in the wind. Somewhere nearby, someone was mowing their lawn. Olive could hear the rumbling sound of the engine in the background. She felt incredibly happy and peaceful. It was as if time had come to a stop, and there were no problems in the world whatsoever. As she sat there and watched, she found herself drifting away. Daydreaming. One moment she was flying high over the earth in the Gizmoblaster, the next she was zooming past the sun. She was falling toward the ocean when her little imaginary *escapade* was interrupted by the voice of her mom.

"Oh, look Olive," said her mom as she pointed out the big window, "your friends are coming."

"Fantastic, they are going to Wizzy Gizmo's with me."

Now, something you should know about the Sanderson's is that they live in the oldest part of Sunnyville, in one of the oldest, little houses just outside town. If you were a stranger passing by you would probably, like most people, stop for a minute just to behold the beauty of that little house. It is a *picturesque* English cottage, which looks like it has been taken from a page in an old storybook and dropped right where it sits, a very long time ago. Olive's favorite part was the big front door that was rounded at the top. As Mrs. Sanderson opened the heavy wooden door to let them in, the *antique* hinges creaked and moaned as if saying, "Nooooo, I'm too ooooold, and too tiiiiiired to do this again." A tall, dark-haired girl, and two boys, one with black hair, and one with brown hair, entered. Summer said, "Hello, Mrs. Sanderson." Eli flashed a shy grin, and Thomas said, "Olive, are you ready to roll?"

"You better believe it!"

Seconds later the four friends were running, laughing, jumping, skipping, and skateboarding their way to Wizzy Gizmo's *eclectic* old workshop. Their imaginations ran wild with thoughts of coming adventures and the expectation that something exciting would occur. What incredible invention would Wizzy Gizmo exhibit today?

CHAPTER 2

Picnic Mayhem

When they arrived at the workshop, Wizzy greeted the kids with a warm smile, and led the *coterie* – which if you don't know is a group of close friends – out back to his garden where Pepe and Qwacky were up to their typical *antics*. Pepe was sprinkling dashes of herbs and spices into a large stockpot. Qwacky was putting what looked like sardines into a blender. There was a small picnic table covered with a variety of foods, many of them unfamiliar to the children.

Pepe bowed low, his tail wagging, his panting now under control, he said, "Buenos dias, mis amigos – which translated means 'good morning, my friends' – I am so pleased you could come." To everyone's delight Pepe showed unusual control, at least, unusual for an incredibly hungry dog that was cooking an incredibly tasty meal. This time, he actually kept his tongue from flapping over the side of his jaw as he spoke. Qwacky, now finished with the sardines, zipped back and forth, his tank-like feet leaving tracks everywhere he went; he called out, "What's a-qwacken?"

"Time to eat!" bellowed Wizzy. Everyone scampered as quickly as they could to the picnic table to get a seat. After a short prayer the children sat down. They were served such a wide variety of tasty, and not-so-tasty foods that they were in turn delighted, disgusted, dismayed, thrilled, and sometimes at a loss to know what manner of food they were **consuming**. The kids struggled not to blast an out loud laugh as they were thoroughly entertained by a fierce duel put on by the fencing spoons. That's when it happened. Qwacky started to jump up and down, lights flashing, alarms sounding, feet kicking. He was holding onto his bill with both hands. He looked like his head was about to explode.

"What is happening Qwacky?" said the kids with great concern.

Qwacky answered with a strange nasally voice, "I, I, I, t-t-t-tink I got a piece of c-c-c-carrot stuck in my d-n-na-nose."

With a great POOOF, from the greatly distressed duck's nose, a large chunk of carrot shot out, flying across the yard, knocking the dancing toaster right off the table. Like dominoes, the falling toaster started a chain reaction. It landed on Thomas' skateboard, which then flipped up into the air and collided with a stack of books. Books went flying everywhere. One large book knocked the iron off the table. The iron landed on the tail of the skateboard, which had by now settled on the ground. Up, up, up into the air went the skateboard (you know this cannot end well). This time, on its way back down, the skateboard hit the edge of a cutting board sitting on the table. On the cutting board lay three darts, which were minding their own business. "Quick, everybody duck!" yelled Qwacky, as the darts rocketed through the air. There was a loud

clunk as the dartboard fell from the tree to the ground. Everyone stood frozen – afraid to move. Is it over, or is there more? Has the carrot been disarmed? A minute later, when it finally seemed safe, they relaxed, and let out a collective sigh of relief. Fortunately, no one was hurt. Thomas walked over to the dartboard, picked it up, and in complete astonishment, turned to Qwacky and said, "Look at this! You hit the bull's eye, Qwacky."

Qwacky couldn't believe his eyes. He yelled out, "Qwack-a-doodle-doo!"

They all gathered around the table and were amazed that none of their plates had been disturbed by the disastrous **mayhem** Qwacky's carrot nose blasting had caused.

When everyone had eaten until they could eat no more, a very large and mischievous grin began to form on Wizzy Gizmo's face. Finally, he asked, "Would you kid's like to see my new invention?"

There was a resounding, "YES!" from all the children.

CHAPTER 3

Wondrous and Tasty Inventions

Wizzy took the kids over to a large lumpy pile and removed an old paint-splattered tarp, which concealed his new invention. "Wow! ... What is it?" asked Thomas.

"I call it the Gizmogardengomatic," Wizzy said.

What they saw was a giant yellow metal box **situated** on top of an old rickety wheelbarrow. A rake hung down to the ground at the back of the contraption. A green garden hose drooped over the back of the wheelbarrow, like a tail. Wizzy dumped a bag of carrot seeds into the funnel shaped hopper, which looked like a giant ice cream cone. This hopper had a wide mouth at the top and then narrowed down into a small tube at the bottom. Then, Wizzy opened a small door in the front of the contraption, and put a bunch of carrots inside. **Hordes** of hairy, hungry, hamsters were happily hanging out inside, and when they saw the carrots, they all began running around excitedly. This made the wheels and gears, which propelled the Gizmogardengomatic, rotate and spin. The machine lurched forward slowly. As it rolled along it made little holes in the ground, deposited seeds, covered the seeds, and watered the mounds. Suddenly it came to a stop.

"What happened Wizzy?"

Wizzy was now hunched over his new invention, tinkering with this and that, turning knobs and making adjustments. He scratched his head, further messing up his disheveled bluish-hair, pushed his thick black glasses back up the bridge of his nose, looked at the kids with a **contorted** smile, and said with a chuckle, "It's almost a perfect self-gardening machine. The only problem is that the hamsters eat more carrots than I can possibly grow."

Ha! Ha! Ha! The kids laughed, and Olive said affectionately, "I think it is a great invention." Wizzy laughed too.

"At least it keeps the hamsters well-fed and exercised."

Wizzy walked over to his workbench and picked up a big wooden bucket-like thing from a shelf. It had black, green, and white wires going in and out, and a metal spout sticking out the front. There was a big handle up on top and a crank sticking out of the side. The whole thing was covered in frost. Placing it on the table he said, "Can anybody guess what this does?"

"I know, I know," shouted Thomas, "it's a garbage compactor."

Eli said, with an air of authority, "It's a watering can."

Olive, expertly said, "It is a fruit juice maker."

"Incorrect my friends, I call it the Gizmoanycream. Just put something in, turn the crank a few times, and ice cream comes out."

"Amazing," said Summer, in awe of Wizzy's *ingenuity*.

She poured her lemonade into the hole at the top, and turned the crank round and round. The machine hissed, whined, clanked, popped, and a few dozen crank *revolutions* later, with a loud plop, out came lemonade ice cream. Thomas used chocolate milk, Olive used orange juice, and Eli, overcome with curiosity, made salad dressing ice cream.

The salad dressing ice cream was interesting, and Qwacky dubbed it, "The most interesting, and delightful ice cream in the world."

Summer just called it, "Gross."

"Wow!" exclaimed Thomas, both grossed and impressed. He was *flabbergasted* that you could turn almost anything into ice cream at a moment's notice. "How did you ever get to be so creative?" he asked.

Wizzy laughed, his blue eyes twinkling, "It's not just me that is creative. Let me tell you about some incredibly talented and creative people who lived a long, long time ago."

Creative Like the Creator

Everybody gathered around as Wizzy opened his Bible. He said, "A good example of man's artistic creativity is shown to us in Exodus 35:30-35. Listen to what it says,

> 'Then Moses said to the sons of Israel, "'See, the LORD has called by name Bezalel the son of Uri, the son of Hur, of the tribe of Judah. And He has filled him with the Spirit of God, in wisdom, in understanding and in knowledge and in all craftsmanship; to make designs for working in gold and in silver and in bronze, and in the cutting of stones for settings and in the carving of wood, so as to perform in every inventive work. He also has put in his heart to teach, both he and Oholiab, the son of Ahisamach, of the tribe of Dan. He has filled them with skill to perform every work of an engraver and of a designer and of an embroiderer, in blue and in purple and in scarlet material, and in fine linen, and of a weaver, as performers of every work and makers of designs.""
>
> **Exodus 35:30-35**

You see kids; God gave the people of the nation of Israel the necessary skills to build the tabernacle, the earthly home for God to be with His people. He gave them both the technical and the artistic skills needed to make the tabernacle a thing of wonder and beauty. The various items used in the manufacture and design of the tabernacle, such as gold, silver, and bronze, as well as the way things worked in it, were meant to be symbolic of spiritual truths. Not only that, the tabernacle was also designed to be portable."

"Portable? You mean it was like the first motor home ever built?" asked Thomas. He was thinking about his grandfather's great big motor home. It was almost as long as his parents house and had a kitchen, a bath and stripes that ran across the sides.

Wizzy chuckled, "Well, not exactly Thomas. The important thing to recognize here is that all of that work took a great deal of creative skill and design. All of which was possible only because God had created these artists and architects in His image, and He gave them the abilities and skills to get the job done, just right. Being creative is one of the ways people reflect God's image. Remember last time, through the wonder of Gizmovision we explored the Bible's book of Genesis, and we saw that God made man in His own image?"

"Yes, I remember," said Summer.

"Good Summer, you will remember then that Genesis 1:26 says, 'Let Us make man in Our image, and after Our likeness.' Does anyone remember what that means?"

"I think I know," said Eli, "it means that God made us like Him in many ways. And when He created man, it was a unique and special process different from the rest of creation. That is why when He created everything else He said, 'And let there be', but when He created man He said, 'Let Us make.'"

"Exactly," said Wizzy beaming at the brown-haired boy.

"What about that part when He said, 'In Our likeness?'" asked Olive.

"Well Olive, that is another way man is different from the rest of creation. When God formed man He not only made man in His own image but also in His likeness, and He breathed into man the breath of life. You see, God was **intimately** involved in the creation of man. And man is not only creative like God, he is also an eternal being with an eternal soul. This is why man has a special relationship with God that is different from the rest of creation."

"Wow! That is amazing," said Olive.

"It sure is. Can you guys give me more examples of how man is different from the rest of creation?"

"Well," **ventured** Summer, knitting her dark eyebrows into a thoughtful expression, "people can think in complicated ways. Like creating languages so we can read and write, and exploring mathematics so we can learn how to count and use numbers."

"Oh Wow!" said Qwacky, "I just realized that I am an example of man's incredible ingenuity. To be more specific, Wizzy's ingenuity. Wizzy designed me, built me and programmed me to be incredibly fast at computing things like algebra, trigonometry, statistics, calculus, astrophysics, and more importantly, where to find the bacon."

To which Pepe replied, "I like bacon."

Everyone laughed.

"Yes!" Wizzy answered with enthusiasm. "I can think **logically** and **rationally** because God made me in His own image. We humans are rational, creative, and inventive because God is rational, creative, inventive, and He has given us this ability as well."

"*Precisely!*" said Thomas with a grin. "That's why we can invent motorcycles, race cars, airplanes, scramjets, rockets, super-sonic-hyper-drive-extra-terrestrial-deep-space-galactic-light-speed-…"

"That boy has a need for speed!" said Qwacky, as he zoomed back and forth around the garden knocking over a variety of squash, and the occasional head of cabbage.

"What about beautiful things like pretty dresses, scrapbooks, poetry, paintings, and musicals? These things show people's creativity and inventiveness too, don't they," said Olive looking **askance** at the boys.

Pepe interrupted and began singing, "A spoonful of sugar helps the medicine go down…," in his deep throaty voice as he strummed on an imaginary guitar. He was quite good, considering the average dog does not play the guitar.

The kids laughed.

"I think my favorite inventions are cheeseburgers, fries, and chocolate milkshakes," said Eli licking his lips. You may have noticed that napkins and showers did not make the list.

"Keep in mind strawberry and blackberry shakes!" said Summer as she tilted her head towards Eli and flashed a correcting look his way.

"My *preference* is cheesecake with raspberry sauce," thought Olive.

"Those are all great observations," said Wizzy, "mankind has invented and created so many different things because we are made in the image of God. Now there's one last thing I want you kids to notice, in this passage we see the first introduction of the Trinity. The Hebrew word used here for God, Elohim, is plural, and that means that while there is but one living and true God, He eternally exists in three persons, Father, Son and Holy Spirit – each equally deserving worship, and obedience. It is a sort of three-in-oneness. This is a mystery to us all."

"Are you kids ready for another Gizmovision adventure?" asked Wizzy.

A *cacophony* of responses came out all at once. It sounded something like, yeah let's do, it it's about time, let's roll, or something to that effect.

In His Image?

CHAPTER 5

A Perfect World

Thomas, Eli, Summer, and Olive, in a ***volley*** of excitement, burst through an odd shaped barn-like door, ahead of Wizzy and scurried up to Wizzy Gizmo's incredible invention. Thomas exclaimed, ***sotto voce***, which simply means in a soft voice,

"Gizmovision is sooooo amazing."

Wizzy walked over to his desk and fumbled around looking for his glasses, forgetting they were stuck in the mass of his disheveled bluish-white hair. As he reached up to scratch his head…, "Oh there they are," he chuckled, as he said to the kids, "remember how on our previous Gizmovision ***excursion***, we watched as God created the world, from nothing. ***Theologians***, who are simply people who study God's word, call it ***ex nihilo***, which is Latin for "from nothing." We then saw God create beautiful plants of all types, as well as the sun, the moon, and the stars. God simply said, "Let there be…," and birds, sea creatures, and animals of all kinds, sprang instantly into existence. The animals were incredible; some beautiful, some large, some small, some skinny, some fat, some fast, some slow, red, yellow, black, green, and all the colors of the rainbow. They demonstrated the ***incomprehensible*** creativity of their Maker. There were thousands and thousands of ***species***, each of them with many varieties. Then God did something really amazing, something special, and something distinct. He created man in His image, both male and female. Then He rested."

"Now this is very important, so listen carefully," Wizzy said. "Even though God rested on the seventh day from His work of creation that does not mean that He was tired. Nor does it mean that He quit working completely. In fact, He still works as He is constantly **sustaining** everything. In other words, He keeps everything running smoothly all of the time. If He were to stop doing this, everything would fly apart in total and absolute destruction."

"That would not be good, not be good at all," ventured Qwacky.

"That's right Qwacky. Here is something else that is very, very important. Colossians 1:16 and 17 says that Jesus not only created everything but that He holds it all together as well. This demonstrates the working of the Trinity in creation and in sustaining everything. Let me read those verses to you so you can see it for yourself,

> **'For by Him all things were created, both in the heavens and on earth, visible and invisible, whether thrones or dominions or rulers or authorities—all things have been created through Him and for Him. He is before all things, and in Him all things hold together.'"**
>
> **Colossians 1:16-17**

"Let's get this thing started," said Wizzy as he placed the Bible on his fancy **contraption**, he turned to

Genesis chapter two, and set the marker for verses four through twenty-five. There was a whirl, a hum, some other weird noises, and then a blue-green laser-like light shot out from the top. It curved around in every direction to make a ***translucent***, blue-green bubble surrounding Wizzy, the kids, Pepe, and Qwacky. All at once the workshop and all its noises faded away. They gasped at the beauty of their surroundings.

"Hey, this looks familiar," said Summer, "this is the world right after God created it."

Summer's brown eyes shone as she watched two lions wrestling playfully under the spreading canopy of a magnificent oak tree.

Olive was ***entranced*** as she watched the squirrels play the games they play, and the birds sing from the trees. Even the eagles were soaring, just for the fun of it.

In the middle of this distraction, and ***reverie***, and without warning, a booming voice, which ***elicited*** awe in the listeners, came out of Wizzy's invention with authority and grandeur, and spoke,

> **"This is the account of the heavens and the earth when they were created, in the day that the LORD God made earth and heaven."**
>
> **Genesis 2:4**

"Wow! Can we go on a hike through creation please?" said Olive jumping up and down with excitement. "It's all so pretty."

They walked along, stopping to look at towering trees.

They admired the beautiful flowers. They saw monkeys swinging through trees calling, out to one another, great birds flying high through the air. Deer were grazing in a clearing, and a couple of bears watched with sleepy interest as rabbits hopped around them. They saw stately elk slowly moving in small herds, and a family of large cats running extremely fast as they faded into the distance. There were wild donkeys and horses galloping nearby. This was nature in its perfect state, so much so that it was difficult to take it all in.

Olive stopped to watch a tortoise move s-l-o-w-l-y across the path. She wondered aloud, "I wonder where he is going and why is he so slow?" Getting no answer, she moved on to other interesting things. Other amazing things were close by, far off, and everywhere else as well.

Suddenly Eli piped up, "Hey Wizzy, where are Adam and Eve?" It had dawned on him that they were missing from this wonderful and *idyllic* place.

Pepe wrinkled up his nose sniffing, "I cannot even smell them."

He is a much better sniffer than the kids, as you may or may not know most dogs are that way.

"Let me see," said Qwacky activating his radar, "Hey! They're not anywhere!"

"Oh no! What happened to them? Where did they go?" said Summer with concern in her voice, fearing they had become lost.

"Not to worry kids," answered Wizzy, "this part of the Bible, Genesis chapter two begins on day six."

"Sometimes in those portions of Scripture, we classify as the 'History Books,' some events are recorded in one section of the Bible and then are repeated again later on in another section in greater detail. We call this style of writing, *parallelism*. Now, if you can remember parallelism, you will definitely be able to really impress your friends."

"Rewind to day six!" Qwacky shouted – the way movie directors do while on a set. His voice even had that fantastic sound stage echo.

CHAPTER 6

Plants, Plants, Plants

"This part rewinds so we can take a closer look at how God created mankind," explained Wizzy.

The loud booming voice broke in again,

"Now no shrub of the field was yet on the earth, and no plant of the field had yet sprouted, for the LORD God had not sent rain upon the earth, and there was no man to cultivate the ground."

Genesis 2:5

"Wait a second, did I rewind to the wrong place?" asked Qwacky, spinning furiously, "I thought God created plants on day three. Did I get all twisted up again, Wizzy?"

"No Qwacky, you are not 'twisted up' God did create plants on day three."

"Well then, why does it say there were no plants on day six? Is that a mistake?" asked Qwacky.

Now dizzy from spinning, he teetered, tottered, then fell over with a thud.

"A MISTAKE!" echoed the kids, "not possible!"

"Of course it's not a mistake," said Wizzy, "the Bible

does not contain error. The Bible is God's word, so it is absolutely true! Are you ready for a big word?"

"I'm ready," said Eli. He loves big words.

"The Bible is **inerrant**."

"Inner what?" ***queried*** Qwacky.

"No, not inner, in-err-ant," said Wizzy. "Did you notice that middle part?"

"I got it! I got it!" said Qwacky, "they just scrambled the word, right? In-air-ant, is like, an ant that is in air. You know, like an ant that is flying in the air."

"Ay, Qwacky," said Pepe, "inerrant simply means that the Bible is without error. No mistakes, no contradictions, totally accurate and consistent with itself."

"WOW!" said the kids in unison.

"That's right," said Wizzy. "Getting back to our problem about day six, the answer is actually quite simple. Some of the plants, weeds and thistles, as an example, were to appear after the fall of man, some just needed water. This is revealed to us in Genesis 2:5. There were also different kinds of plants, plants that needed men to labor and toil over them, and rain to water them. The plants God made on day three did not need man to **cultivate** them. So, no mistake here, God's word is faithful and true."

"That makes sense," said Eli, "but how did the plants God created on day three get their water if it didn't rain?"

"Well that is a great question. Let's see what the

Plants, Plants, Plants

Bible says about that," said Wizzy. Genesis 2:6 boomed out,

> **"But a mist used to rise from the earth and water the whole surface of the ground."**
>
> **Genesis 2:6**

"A mist?" said the kids.

"You mean like when it's foggy?" asked Summer.

"Fogs are spooooky!" said Qwacky.

Wizzy and the kids all laughed.

"Actually," said Wizzy, "in Hebrew – which is the language this part of the Bible was originally written in – this word can be translated as a mist. Or, it could also be translated as 'waters from the deep,' which might have been like an underground river, flowing through the rock and dirt."

"Coooool!" said Thomas.

"So, it had not rained yet?" asked Eli.

"Yes, that's right. There was no need for rain because the waters from the deep perfectly provided all the water the trees and plants needed!"

"Muy perfecto," Pepe *observed*.

"It was perfect Pepe," said Wizzy, "there was no need for cultivating or watering the ground, no need for hunting or farming. Plants provided plenty of food, and water came up from the ground. There were no dry deserts or wastelands, no plowing of the fields or waiting for rain. Water was provided in perfect timing."

"Perfection," Qwacky sighed.

"That's right Qwacky, a perfectly watered paradise," said Wizzy. "Let's see what happens next."

CHAPTER 7

In His Image

The Gizmovision voice boomed out,

"Then the LORD God formed man of dust from the ground, and breathed into his nostrils the breath of life; and man became a living being."

Genesis 2:7

Wizzy commented, "Did you notice that Adam is referred to as a 'living *being*?' That's important. It shows that he is seperate from the animals. Did you also notice that he was 'formed from the dust of the ground?' This is important too. It distinguishes him from the uncreated Jehovah."

"Jehovah, who's that," asked Qwacky.

"Jehovah is a name for God which means the self-existent One. Sometimes in Scripture it is explained as, 'I AM THAT I AM.' The name carries the meaning that God is, and always has been, and always will be."

"Look," all of the kids exclaimed together, "there's Adam!"

"The original granddaddy of all," quacked Qwacky. The kids laughed and Pepe shook his head.

Thomas had been looking steadily at Adam with his brow *furrowed*.

"Wait a second," he said finally, "you mean to tell me God made Adam out of dirt?"

"I've always thought you humans had an earthy aroma," noted Pepe.

Eli looked wonderstruck. He couldn't believe that God formed man from the dust of the ground and then breathed into him the breath of life. This not only made Adam a living being, but also made him a spiritual being capable of having fellowship with, and offering service to God. After standing open mouthed for quite a few seconds Eli finally asked,

"Does this mean that we are just living-dirt, like the animals, or is there something special about us?"

"There is definitely something special about man," Wizzy smiled. "God brought all creatures to life, but man is the only creature made in 'the image of God.' Not only that, but man is the only creature that has a soul. Remember God breathed into Adam the breath of life."

Qwacky blasted disco music and sang out, "He's a soul man!"

Wizzy laughed and said, "Yes, God gave people souls. Remember the Bible says that only man is made in God's image. The earth, the stars, the plants, and animals were not created this way! When was the last time you saw a monkey writing poetry, or a cat building a house, or an elephant cooking a burger?"

The kids all laughed as they imagined what the world would be like if animals acted like people. Summer looked around and smiled at the animals that were acting like, well, animals.

Then she was struck by a thought, "Hey, Wizzy, where is Adam going to live? I don't see any houses or buildings."

"Great question," Wizzy chuckled. "Although the whole earth was created good and beautiful, God is about to make man a special home. We need to get a birds-eye view to see it!"

"Don't you mean a ducks-eye view?" **quipped** Qwacky with a grin.

The kids all laughed. "It's time for the Gizmoblaster!" said Wizzy – as he played with the controls on his wrist.

They heard the roar of powerful jet engines. An enormous, red-rocket-car rolled up and stopped in front of the kids. They quickly piled in and **donned** seat belts, because you never knew what Wizzy was going to do. Wizzy got into the driver's seat and began pressing buttons. The engine roared and they were off! Flying through the air, they heard Genesis 2:8 through 10 as though it were in full surround sound,

"And the LORD God planted a garden toward the east, in Eden; and there He placed the man whom He had formed. Out of the ground the LORD God caused to grow every tree that is

pleasing to the sight and good for food; the tree of life also in the midst of the garden, and the tree of the knowledge of good and evil. Now a river flowed out of Eden to water the garden; and from there it divided and became four rivers."

Genesis 2:8-10

The kids were amazed as they looked down at the garden of Eden. They had never seen a place so beautiful before.

"The trees are majestic. They're so tall!" breathed Olive. Her mouth remained open as she tried to ***revel*** in the majesty and delightful beauty of it all.

"Yes, Olive, they are majestic and tall, and... they're filled with perfect, fruity deliciousness!" said Thomas, licking his lips.

Qwacky broke out in song,

"One, two, three,

Look at me,

I'm a-gonna live in an apple tree!"

The sweet smell of fruit, and flowers ***wafted*** up to the Gizmoblaster.

"Can we go down and see the garden paleeeaze?" pleaded Summer.

"Of course!" laughed Wizzy, as he pressed more buttons on the Gizmoblaster guiding it to the ground.

The Gizmoblaster landed with a gentle bump and everyone stepped out into the garden of Eden. The group of friends stood in silence taking in the beauty. After a while Eli noted, "That tree seems different than the others."

"Ah! yes," answered Wizzy, "that is the TREE OF LIFE."

"That is kind of a funny name for a tree," said Thomas.

"That's because it's not a normal tree. Is it, Wizzy?" asked Summer thoughtfully.

Wizzy answered, "Correct! The tree of life is not an average tree, it is a supernatural tree."

"Ah… I get it, I get it," said Qwacky. "Supernatural, that's ah… that's more than natural… that's like ah… natural milk left out in the sun for hours and hours in the heat, and the sun, and the wind, and the rain and all the elements, making it supernatural."

"Ay, Qwacky, that's just disgusting. That's not what supernatural means," said Pepe. "Supernatural means that something **transcends**, that is to say, it is outside the laws of nature."

"What makes that tree supernatural?" said Eli scratching his head.

"Well," said Wizzy, "whoever eats of its fruit, will live forever."

"Forever!" echoed the kids, "wow!"

Pepe interjected, "As a creature with a considerably shorter lifespan, I am all for it."

Wizzy chuckled and said, "Yes, at this point in creation, there was no sin or death. God created man to live forever. The same way God lives forever. This is another way in which people are made in God's image."

Qwacky, who had been enjoying his time by using his tank treads to build a racetrack, and then race around and around, flopped over on the ground exhausted.

Everyone laughed and Thomas said, "This is the coolest place ever. It's perfect."

"Yes! That's exactly what it is Thomas," said Wizzy.

A moment later Eli called out in an excited voice, "Hey Wizzy, I see Adam."

Genesis 2:15 boomed out,

"Then the LORD God took the man and put him in the garden of Eden to cultivate it and keep it."
Genesis 2:15

"Cultivate and keep it, that sounds like work," exclaimed Thomas, "that doesn't sound like paradise."

Wizzy laughed, "Ah, but Adam was not yet affected by sin. So, he never got tired, and work was a joy for him. He enjoyed it just like you enjoy building a skateboard ramp or a gigantic fort."

Pepe wagged his tail excitedly, "You mean, he would

play fetch with me, without ever getting tired, over, and over, and over again. How magnificent that would be."

Olive wondered aloud, "Wizzy, what kind of work did Adam do?"

"Well," answered Wizzy, "one thing we know for certain is that he tended the garden. No doubt, a joy filled task. He also was quite busy naming all the animals."

Genesis chapter 2 verse 20a burst out as if on cue,

"The man gave names to all cattle, and to the birds of the sky, and to every beast of the field …"

Genesis 2:20a

"Wow, it took me a week just to name my puppy," said Olive. "It would take me forever to come up with names for so many creatures."

Qwacky seemed intrigued by the idea and burst out singing,

"Naming the animals one by one,
Naming the animals it must be done.

This one's a bird with its nest so high,
That one's a bird, but it doesn't fly.

The big fuzzy guy we'll call a bear,
He looks very cuddly with so much hair.

Hip-po-pot-amus, now that's a good name,
He smiles from the pool, 'I'm glad you came.'

Animals, animals, great and small,
Animals, animals he must name them all."

The kids all burst out laughing at Qwacky's silly song. Qwacky then gave a deep bow.

After everyone had quieted down, and were watching Adam and the animals walking in the garden, Wizzy spoke up,

"Let's review a little here. What have you learned?"

"God made man in His own image," Summer called out.

"God made a home for Adam in the garden of Eden," added Olive.

Thomas piped up, "Adam worked, but it was fun and filled with joy."

"God planted the tree of life in the garden...but, what's that tree over there?" said Eli, noticing a unique looking tree.

"Oh, yes," said Wizzy, as if he just remembered something very important. "That tree. That is the tree of the knowledge of good and evil!"

The deep voice boomed out Genesis 2:16-17,

"The LORD God commanded the man, saying, 'From any tree of the garden you may eat freely; but from the tree of the knowledge of good

and evil you shall not eat, for in the day that you eat from it you will surely die.'"

Genesis 2:16-17

"Die!" said Thomas, his voice full of surprise, "that's not good."

"Not good at all," answered Summer, "what an evil tree."

Wizzy rubbed his wild blue-hair making it stick up even higher. "Actually," he said, "the Bible say's everything God made was good, so the tree itself was good, not evil. It's disobeying God that is evil."

Thomas scrunched up his face thinking hard. "So, is that what sin means then; disobeying God?"

"That's exactly right," answered Wizzy.

The sound of running broke the somber mood of the group.

"Who's that?" asked Eli, surprised.

"It's Adam," shouted Thomas, "he can really run."

The group watched Adam disappear out of sight behind a group of trees with amazing speed.

"I bet he could really throw a ball," *postulated* Eli.

"I do not think I want to play fetch anymore!" joked Pepe, "I would get tired long before Adam would."

Wizzy laughed at Pepe, and gave him an affectionate pat. "That's right, without sin man was an amazing creation."

"Olive, what's wrong?" asked Wizzy, looking down into Olive's face. Her green eyes were full of sadness.

"It's just that, well, Adam is all alone. There's no one to be his friend or for him to talk to, or to work with, it's really quite sad," she said with a l-o-n-g sigh.

"Well, he could talk to the animals," Thomas suggested, looking up at a monkey chattering away in a nearby tree.

"Yes. But, that's not going to *suffice*," answered Pepe. He knew that talking with a dog, even one that would sit and look into his eyes, giving the impression he knew what Adam was saying, was not what Adam needed.

"We know that God made Adam to be a relational being; to share his thoughts, ideas, and emotions with God and other humans. Being alone was a big problem. So God did something really amazing."

"What is that?" asked all the kids simultaneously.

"He made the first woman," answered Wizzy with a smile.

The Gizmovision device boomed out,

"Then the LORD God said, 'It is not good for the man to be alone; I will make him a helper suitable for him.' Out of the ground the LORD God formed every beast of the field and every bird of the sky, and brought them to the man to see

> what he would call them; and whatever the man called a living creature, that was its name. The man gave names to all the cattle, and to the birds of the sky, and to every beast of the field, but for Adam there was not found a helper suitable for him. So the LORD God caused a deep sleep to fall upon the man, and he slept; then He took one of his ribs, and closed up the flesh at that place. The LORD God fashioned into a woman the rib which He had taken from the man, and brought her to the man."
>
> **Genesis 2:18-22**

The kids watched in amazement as Adam went to sleep, and God fashioned the woman from Adam's rib. Then they saw God bring her to Adam.

"Wow, she's so beautiful," whispered Olive.

"Is that Eve?" asked Summer.

"Yes," replied Wizzy, "but Adam did not actually name her Eve until later. However, we can call her Eve now, if you would like." The voice continued,

> "The man said,
> 'This is now bone of my bones,
> And flesh of my flesh;
> She shall be called Woman,
> Because she was taken out of Man.'"
>
> **Genesis 2:23**

"That sounds like a poem or something," said Summer, hugging herself.

"Yes, in fact, you could say it's the very first love song," said Wizzy. He launched into one of his teaching moments, "Notice that she was not made from the dirt as Adam was. She was made from a portion of Adam, because she was made for an ***inseparable*** unity and fellowship with Adam. The ***mode*** of her creation was to lay the foundation for the ***morality*** of marriage. Being made from Adam's side was to illustrate she is to stand beside him as a helper."

Qwacky pretended to play the violin as he sang, "You are bone of my bones, flesh of my flesh."

"I think it loses something in the translation," said Pepe, as everyone laughed.

"Hmm," said Wizzy ***mussing*** up his hair, again, "well it's important to understand that Adam is expressing the idea of family. Adam is saying to her, 'You are my family.' That was even before they had children. In fact, the way God designed the family, only the relationship between a man and woman is permanent. Children grow up and start a new family. As the children reach maturity they are to leave and start their own families. Does anyone know the name we give this relationship between a man and woman, a husband and wife?"

"I know! I know! It's called being in wuv," blurted Qwacky. He grabbed Pepe by the arms and spun him in waltz-like circles. Pepe did everything he could to wiggle and squirm out of Qwacky's grasp. It was such a funny sight the kids laughed and giggled hysterically.

After all the giggling had stopped Wizzy answered, "Well, love is a very important part of it, but the word I'm looking for starts with an m and rhymes with carriage."

"MARRIAGE," all the kids yelled together.

"You got it," said Wizzy.

Amazed, Summer asked, "There was marriage in the beginning?"

Wizzy smiled, "Yes, from the very beginning, God designed and **ordained** marriage as a unique relationship between one man and one woman. It was through this relationship that the earth would become populated." That is why God declared,

> **"For this reason a man shall leave his father and his mother, and be joined to his wife; and they shall become one flesh."**
> **Genesis 2:24**

Eli looked a bit stunned, "But Wizzy, what if they get mad at each other and don't want to be around each other anymore?"

"What if the man is too stinky?" said Olive.

"Or the woman is too hairy?" added Thomas.

"What is wrong with hairy?" asked Pepe, pretending to be offended. "Hairy is good."

"Well," said Wizzy, "God intended for marriage to be for life. In fact, another passage in the Bible, Matthew 19:5-6 says,

> **'…Have you not read that He who created them from the beginning MADE THEM MALE**

AND FEMALE, and said, "FOR THIS REASON A MAN SHALL LEAVE HIS FATHER AND MOTHER AND BE JOINED TO HIS WIFE, AND THE TWO SHALL BECOME ONE FLESH"? So they are no longer two, but one flesh. What therefore God has joined together let no man separate.'"

Matthew 19:5-6

"They are no longer two, but one body," explained Wizzy. "You don't get rid of your feet because they are stinky, or your arms because they are hairy, do you?" Wizzy asked, his blue eyes twinkling.

The kids laughed at the ridiculous question.

Wizzy continued, "God intended marriage to be a lifelong relationship. It is a good, and precious gift from God, and it reflects His character."

"I guess it is a good thing God did not leave Adam alone," said Summer.

"Yes," added Olive excitedly. "Now Adam has someone to talk to, to love and he can enjoy life with her. Not only that, they can have children, and those children can grow up, get married and have more children, and those children grow up, get married and have more children, and those children grow up, get married and have more children…"

"We get the idea Olive," interrupted Wizzy laughing. "Here in the beginning, you see God's design for the family."

"Yes, that's what I meant," said Olive with a grin.

"Hey, Wizzy," said Thomas.

"Yes Thomas," replied Wizzy.

"I was just thinking about how Adam named all of the animals. How he named Eve, and how God told him to cultivate the garden. It almost seems like Adam was responsible for, and in charge of, a lot of things. Is that true?"

"Those are fantastic observations Thomas. You are absolutely right. Here at the very beginning God set in place a system of authority. God is in control of everything because He created everything, but He also gave Adam and Eve responsibility and authority too. That's why He said in Genesis chapter 1 and verse 28, they were to 'subdue the earth and rule over the animals.' Adam demonstrated this authority when he named the animals and Eve. Both Adam and Eve demonstrated it in ruling over the earth. Theologians have a fancy word for it. Adam and Eve are called *vice-regents*. They are under God, and over the earth."

"I think we have one more verse in this passage," said Wizzy. The voice boomed out in reply,

"And the man and his wife were both naked and were not ashamed."
                                    Genesis 2:25

"Naked! That doesn't sound very modest, Wizzy," said Summer, blushing a bit.

"Yes," added Thomas "and they weren't even

ashamed!"

"Yes, and without fur, they must get a little bit chilly. No?" *mused* Pepe thoughtfully.

"Well," Wizzy said, "you need to remember that sin had not yet entered the world. Neither Adam nor Eve had rebelled or disobeyed God, so there was nothing to be ashamed of, and Pepe," he added looking at the dog, "the weather must have been quite pleasant in a sinless creation too, so they wouldn't have been too cold or too hot. Everything was just right."

"That really is something," said Summer.

"Amazing," added Olive.

"Yes, I guess it is pretty amazing," said Wizzy. "God created man in His image, male and female, gave them a perfect home and a perfect purpose."

"Do you remember the purpose for which God created us?"

"Man's chief end is to glorify God and enjoy Him forever," all of the kids recited together, remembering what they had learned on their last Gizmovision adventure.

"Wow, you have great memories," said Wizzy.

"That's it for today," said Wizzy. "Let's get back into the Gizmoblaster and take one last look at the garden of Eden."

They all squeezed into the vehicle. Wizzy hit the throttle. The engines roared, and within seconds they were hovering high above the garden. The kids, Wizzy, Qwacky, and Pepe, all peered out at the beautiful landscape. Thomas leaned back in his seat and said,

"I think when we get back I am going to explore my God-given creativity and make some more ice cream."

"As long as it isn't salad dressing flavored," pleaded Summer.

As everyone laughed, Eli thought to himself, "How will we ever top this trip? I wonder what we will learn next time?"

"Hold on everyone, unfortunately it is time to go back to the shack," said Wizzy.

He fiddled with the buttons on the control panel strapped to his wrist. Suddenly, the trees, the animals, the rivers, and everything below started to fade away. There was a shimmer of light all around, and then suddenly, they were back in the Gizmo Shack.

"Wow! That was a fantastic adventure," said Olive. "I can't wait for another chance to explore the Bible."

"Never fear my dear friend, Gizmovision will always be here," said Wizzy with a smile. "There are many more fantastic adventures ahead."

The End
(Actually we are just getting started.)

Review Questions

All right, kids, time to put on your thinking caps. Let us see how much you remember.

Question: What four things did the Spirit of God give Bezalel?
Answer: Wisdom, understanding, knowledge and craftsmanship. Exodus 35:30-35.

Question: The Bible says that God created man in His what?
Answer: God created man in His image and likeness. Genesis 1:26.

Question: What does Trinity mean?
Answer: Trinity means that while there is but one living and true God He eternally exists in three persons, Father, Son and Holy Spirit. Page 23

Question: When God rested from His creative work on the seventh day, did He quit working completely?
Answer: No. He still works as He is constantly sustaining everything. Page 26 Colossians 1:16, 17.

Question: What part did Jesus have in the Creation?
Answer: Jesus both created, sustains, and holds together everything. Colossians 1:16, 17.

Question: What is literary parallelism?
Answer: Literary parallelism is a style of writing where you repeat an event a second time to explain it in more detail. Page 31

REVIEW

Question: What does it mean that the Bible is inerrant?
Answer: When we say the Bible is inerrant we mean that the Bible is without error. No mistakes, no contradictions, totally accurate and consistent with itself. Page 34

Question: What did God make man from?
Answer: God formed man from the dust of the ground. Genesis 2:7

Question: Why did God create man?
Answer: God created man to glorify Him and enjoy Him forever. Page 52

 Now, think of three questions of your own, the harder the better. It's okay if you have to look up the answer.

Vocabulary

antics – silly pranks
antique – made long ago
askance – with doubt or suspicion
cacophony – harsh mixture of sounds
collective – shared by all
consuming – to eat up; devour
contorted – twist bend out of shape
contraption – device or machine
coterie – a small exclusive group
cultivate – prepare the land, nurture something
donned – put on
eclectic – assorted, diverse
elicited – to draw out a response
entranced – to hold somebody's attention and produce a sense of wonder
escapade – adventure, mission, incident
ex nihilo – from or out of nothing
excursion – short trip
flabbergasted – astonished someone utterly
furrowed – wrinkle on the forehead, as a result of frowning
horde – swarm or pack
idyllic – serenely beautiful, wonderful
incomprehensible – beyond understanding
inerrant – incapable of making mistakes
ingenuity – inventiveness
inseparable – so linked as to be impossible to consider separately
intimately – close personal connection
logically – of or according to the rules of logic
mayhem – absolute chaos or severe disruption
mode – manner or form
morality – conformity to the law of God

Vocabulary

mused – a state of deep thought
mussing – mess up, or to mess up someone's hair
observed – notice something, watch carefully
ordained – established, or instituted
parallelism – the expression of an idea in two or more ways
picturesque – attractive, beautiful, lovely, scenic, charming, quaint, pleasing
postulated – assumed something to be true
precisely – exactly, accurately; clearly
preference – liking one thing over another
queried – to ask something as a question
quipped – a witty remark, especially one made on the spur of the moment
rationally – reasonable and sensible; in accordance with reason and logic
revel – enjoy, delight in
reverie – pleasant contemplation
revolution – complete circular turn
simultaneous – at the same time
situated – located
sotto voce – intentionally lowering the volume of one's voice for emphasis
species – family, or breed
suffice – to be enough for somebody
sustaining – to make something continue to exist
theologians – an expert, or student of, theology
transcends – to be independent of the world, to exist above and apart from the world
translucent – glowing; letting through light diffusely
ventured – dare to do or say something
vice-regent – a person who acts in the name of another
volley – simultaneous expression of something
wafted – to float gently through the air

Explore the world of Wizzy Gizmo
and all of his friends at

WWW.WIZZYGIZMO.COM

NEXT IN THIS SERIES

Book Three

The Lost Garden

www.ingramcontent.com/pod-product-compliance
Lightning Source LLC
Chambersburg PA
CBHW040458240426

43665CB00039B/81